I0086677

Praise for
Do Unto Earth

"A must-read book for everyone who cares about the future of humanity and our planet."

> —**Dr. Ervin Laszlo**, two-time Nobel Peace Prize nominee, recipient of the Goi Peace Prize and International Mandir of Peace Prize, best-selling author of Science and the Akashic Field, founder of the Laszlo Institute of New Paradigm Research and The Club of Budapest, fellow of the World Academy of Art and Science and the International Academy of Philosophy of Science

"A 911 call from Planet Earth herself, *Do Unto Earth* is a potent manifesto for living life today and forward. This book should be required reading in schools. We must act now!"

> —**Mary Madeiras**, three-time Emmy-Winning director, screenwriter, Akashic Records practitioner, activist, and author

"*Do Unto Earth* is full of empowering messages and mind-bending assertions that you won't find in science or history textbooks. Given the urgent need for new solutions on this endangered planet, the ideas are worthy of further investigation."

—**Mark Gober**, author of *An End to Upside Down Thinking*, board of directors of the Institute of Noetic Sciences (IONS) and the School of Wholeness and Enlightenment (SoWE)

"From page one, I was hooked! *Do Unto Earth* merges spirituality with our environmental crisis and does it in a way that is as gripping as a blockbuster movie. Brava to Hayes, Borgens … and Pax."

—**Temple Hayes**, author, spiritual leader, animal activist, and founder of illli.org

"The channeled Spirit energy Pax states that we are at the 'crossroads of our survival' and offers us bold envisioning and direction. Mother Earth is speaking, and ancient mysteries are revealed! Let's heed and implement these game-changers for the benefit of us all."

—**Sunny Chayes**, social/human rights and environmental activist, feature writer and Chief Strategic Partner for Whole Life Times, and host of ABC's *Solutionary Sundays*

"Timely, high-level and generative wisdom detailing how we may still sustain our beautiful planet while reclaiming our collective and individual sovereignty."

—**Stephan McGuire**, director of Zürich-based NGO Cernunnos Media, Director of Tree Media Foundation

Pax and Enviro-Tech Gamechangers

Pax and Enviro-Tech Gamechangers

Volume 3 of Do Unto Earth

PENELOPE JEAN HAYES,
CAROLE SERENE BORGENS

Waterside Productions

Copyright © 2020 By Penelope Jean Hayes with
Carole Serene Borgens as channeler

www.PenelopeJeanHayes.com
www.CaroleSereneBorgens.com
www.PaxWisdom.com

All rights reserved. This book or any portion thereof
may not be reproduced or used in any manner whatsoever
without the express written permission of the publisher
except for the use of brief quotations in articles and book
reviews.

Cover design by:
Andrew Green
Books & Illustration

Printed in the United States of America

First Printing, 2020

ISBN-13: 978-1-951805-07-4 print edition
ISBN-13: 978-1-951805-08-1 ebook edition

Waterside Productions
2055 Oxford Ave
Cardiff, CA 92007
www.waterside.com

For you—
so you know for certain that you are the change and
you have the power

Contents

Introduction · xi

Volume 3 · **1**

Do Unto Earth   **Pax and Enviro-Tech**
                          Gamechangers · · · · · · · 1

Chapter Seven: Contact · · · · · · · · · · · · · · 3
Chapter Eight: Oil and Water · · · · · · · · · 21
Chapter Nine: Future Devices 38

About the Author and Channeler· · · · · · · · · · · · · · 49

Introduction

*D*o *Unto Earth* is an extraordinary conversation intended to quantum leap us forward in our spiritual evolution and journey to enlightenment. This message is not a directive delivered from a thousand feet up; this is a very personal message from and dialogue with the Divine Wisdom Source directly to you and for you. Please accept this gift with eyes clear and wide and open.

Within these pages is the blueprint for environmental repair and peace and unity on Earth, however, this booklet constitutes just one of eight volumes that together make up that blueprint. While we believe that the eight topics, as separated by these volumes, are to be understood as connected to each other and only together give the full message as intended, we also understand some readers prefer to focus on their specific areas of interest—hence these eight mini-books by volumes. (Note: Chapters within this volume are numbered as they originally appeared in the book's full-length version.)

As you begin this journey, you might like to know how this collaboration of writing began.

It is indeed my great joy and honor to communicate with the Spirit Messenger, Pax, channeled by Carole Serene Borgens. From a young age, Carole, a former nurse, diligently studied all things metaphysical. This Spirit Messenger first visited her in the early 1990s when she was new to channeling by automatic writing. When her pen wrote the opening introduction and request for her to be a channel, she recognized the profound responsibility attached and jumped up from her office chair to pace the floor—not easy with three sleeping Irish Wolfhounds covering the carpet. Carole's initial response was to ask if she could think about it and take some time to respond, which she was given. Asking, "Why me?" Spirit responded to her: "You are new to this, you have no bad habits, and you will change none of my words." In time, Carole came to be comfortable with this blessing and so began her journey.

I, too, have been a seeker and spiritualist since my years as a teenaged runaway, and so it is a useful tool at times for me to reach out to a reputable intuitive for deeper guidance. Beginning on the fourth of February 2019, I had several long-distance Spirit channeling sessions with Carole—she was in British Columbia and I was in Florida. I had copious questions for Spirit as I sought further direction for my second title, *Do Unto Earth* (which, incidentally, is also the name of my business), while building upon the message of my first title, *The Magic of Viral Energy*. I was expanding and broadening the message of "viral energy" from personal and interpersonal goals to global concerns facing humanity and Planet Earth. I was also simultaneously establishing the Viral Energy Institute, a learning and research platform for the study of Viralenology.

Through our talks, this Spirit Messenger and I were getting to know each other and Spirit felt my passion for the plight of abused animals and species extinction, as well as my intention to bring awareness to our environmental crisis and to share the impacts of "viral energy masses"—large energetic fields created by both light and heavy intentions and action by communities, populations, industries, governments, and cultural beliefs—on Planet Earth. These disruptive energy masses create massive vibrational pockets of particular energies including love, hate, peace, discord, gratitude, violence, forgiveness, indifference, and compassion.

The Spirit Messenger seemed very interested in this direction and before long, Carole contacted me to say that Spirit wished to offer wisdom to be used by and shared through the Viral Energy Institute regarding this mission of planetary healing.

The writing began on the second of October 2019 when I sent questions to Carole who then channeled Spirit's responses by automatic writing (today, she does this via typing). It was *during* the writing that it became clear to all that this conversation would take book form and adopt the title *Do Unto Earth*.

As the answers were returned from Spirit, Carole and I both had many moments of excitement and more than a few gasps followed by, "Ooooh crikey, this is going to change everything!" The first of such revelations came in Chapter One when I asked the Spirit Messenger (whom self-identified with the moniker

PENELOPE JEAN HAYES, CAROLE SERENE BORGENS

"**Pax**", meaning peace) to be more specific about who they are. Here was the answer…

> "We are one with the Universe, not the Universe alone. We are the Divine Universe, yes, and the God being and the greater wisdom, that which knows and supports all and is healing, non-judgmental and tolerant, all-seeing, all-knowing, and Peace."

Volume 3

Do Unto Earth
Pax and Enviro-Tech
Gamechangers

"The only thing that scares me more than space aliens is the idea that there aren't any space aliens. We can't be the best that creation has to offer. I pray we're not all there is. If so, we're in big trouble."

Ellen DeGeneres

American comedian, television host, vegan, and animal rights activist

Chapter Seven

Contact

*W*hile this next question might seem extraneous, it's indeed one of our long-standing enigmas and so I need to ask you: In 1947, did aliens actually crash at Roswell, New Mexico; perhaps one of our friends from another galaxy? If so, what was their purpose or mission to be here rather than to only buzz by?

Buzzing by is what they did regularly, and for this craft to not make it beyond where it came down was an anomaly. It did land where people today believe it did, and the immediate action of cover-up caused the mystery that remains with you now.

Yes, there was knowledge by the government and military that contact was being made, very quietly, and the secretive nature of that was never divulged. Military engineers were building propulsion systems they felt could take them off-planet at a rate and to a distance previously not considered. They had help from the "visitors" and when this flight termination occurred it proved a disaster to that program.

The recovery of craft and personnel did take place, reverse engineering has been considered as motivation, as well as preventing civilian knowledge of the event. There is less secrecy now about visitors' crafts seen on your radar, but aside from that the mystery remains as intended.

(I'm stunned here as this brings alien existence very close to home in a very tangible way, yet decidedly I am deploying a journalism technique borrowed from cards: poker face. The reality is that our United States government still officially claims that the Roswell craft was a weather balloon.)

As motivation for what?

Motivation for engineers to get on with projects designed to take men to interstellar travel more easily. They had their own ideas and plans, but the ability to examine what came in from outside, unexpectedly, was a perfect opportunity to expedite the process.

Did any of the intergalactic visitors survive the crash? And if so, did the United States government keep them alive for a period of time?

Survival might have been the case for one, but the underlying thought of the time was to learn what made these beings able to travel as they did, therefore a certain amount of experimentation was carried out. Testing, it was, as you would test a body for its ability to function under stress. This did not bode well for the survival and it was not to be. Compassion was in place with some, but the process of testing took on new energy when the military might of the time was put in question and those who thought they could say they were enabled to travel intergalactically had to prove that statement. This escalated exploration of the visitors and their craft, and the end came for the visitor as a result.

I am sad for this visitor who died in our possession. I would like to say how sorry I am, on behalf of our people, that we did not help and care for this being who was alive after the crash and could have survived to return home. May you please tell me the name of this individual? Did the spacecraft's crew have families that mourned for them and miss them still (it wasn't that long ago)? Can I send the families a message, through you maybe, if that's possible? I'd like to tell them: "I love you. I'm sending thoughts of light energy to you."

As you have the ability to do so, you may send your thoughts, these thoughts to those close to the crew members who did not make it home. Names are not shared; names are not required in this process or needed for you to extend your sadness at this piece of history that played out in your country.

Can I also send my thoughts to our ET friends of a desire to collaborate with them, now? Friendly intergalactic visitors and their wisdom are needed now to propel our clean energy and clean travel forward. May I invite them to come visit me and help with the mission to heal Earth?

Certainly, you may invite them to collaborate in a telepathic communication. While there may not be instant response, know that if you "tune-in" to them and they to you, ideas will transmit. This is the way of it going forward. More may develop at a later time but for now, this.

I will send them my mind-made invitation, and I do hope that more develops at a later time. I'd be rather interested to meet some of our friendly interstellar visitors; to learn from them and to show them love.

Where are the bodies now of those who crashed at Roswell?

Burned, cremated as evidence was removed ultimately and records kept were also altered from their original form.

Was their spacecraft also destroyed or does any of this technology remain somewhere today?

Ah yes, pieces of this craft were recovered and transported to where they could be examined in detail. It was the need for reverse engineering that kept the secret. There is evidence of this and remaining pieces in secure and in locked vaults in the place where it was all stored originally. Much was destroyed but some know that pieces still remain.

This place is the United States Air Force facility in Nevada called "Area 51", correct?

Yes, and this place remains a safeguard against public knowledge of current projects to develop means of travel to space, and specifically to land and set up housekeeping on another planet.

What is the reason for secrecy?

We say there is consideration of national supremacy on your Earth. As there is much competition for being the first, it becomes about staking territory, planting the flag first and claiming the planet. It already is about divisiveness and supreme power and not about inclusivity and collaboration. There must be the need to be first to the target? This leaves out the option of doing more and better, sooner, and with less expenditure to any one nation. Unfortunately, this level of collaboration seems left to your children who understand the value. Of all the instincts driving your Earth people, greed appears high on the list.

Yes, we are a society largely motivated by greed, a desire to be better than or above others, and a thirst for control over others. Frankly, it's embarrassing—how ridiculous we must appear to

our enlightened ET visitors and onlookers from the Spirit World.

Let's please finish our talk about Area 51 and why the clean-tech knowledge from our interstellar visitors has not been utilized.

There was a sense of fear surrounding this project; fear that more visitors would land, and the knowledge of the time was that the military was no match for what might come. The 1947 landing was a crash—it was felt that if it was followed by a landing of intact craft and crews, there could be no equality in resources or abilities. Fear, again, was responsible for much of the overriding beliefs and actions of government and military officials, as they expected a warring group of extraterrestrials to descend and take over Earth, beginning with the corner inhabited by Area 51. Had these officials thought of a landing and meeting of visitors and hosts as peaceful, and simply interested to learn the fate of their craft and crew, history would show a very different outcome. And, of course, the spinoff is that where there could have been collaboration and learning from the visitors about how their propulsion systems worked and how the construction of their craft could be replicated, there was a missed opportunity. How many decades did this set back the space travel program? Unfortunate, it was, that those in command functioned in fear. This is a lesson for today in your world. To not fear the unknown, but rather respect and take from it what is beneficial while giving what can be shared, is the way.

These visitors who crashed at Roswell: what is their home planet called, and in what galaxy is it located? I can imagine that there are—still—many beings and races of peoples from many planets in many Universes. Is this true?

Yes, this is true, and be aware that names of planets and galaxies that you may know are not a part of this discussion. All things do not bear divulging, as all things are not named, as is your planetary custom. We shall keep this for another time and place.

I just had a thought: Pax, are the friendly visitors who came to help bring us advanced technologies and then crashed at Roswell our relatives—the very same ancestors who so long ago assisted to deliver us to Planet Earth?

Not at all as there are numerous interstellar visitations underway.

The visitors in this experience were of a further galaxy and this makes it even more curious that the craft malfunctioned as it did. It is the case that they were from distance and did not intend to stay.

So, they were of a "further galaxy" to the ones from where we originated when we were starseeded to Earth.

Are all interstellar visitors friendly?

Yes, indeed, and their intention equally friendly and their wish to observe and interact also. There was a higher purpose to this mission. We say it was known they were to visit that day and there was a plan to come together for information sharing. Your military knows this and declassified records, still well buried, will show this and more.

Area 51 it is said, is the place where communication with other planets was being attempted and where craft that could make a voyage into space was in development.

That the visitors chose to contribute technology was a consideration, but did they? It would have been a friendly intention, if so. And have others done so previously, or since this experience, we say it is so.

You say that the United States government was attempting communication with other planets, and that this was being done out of Area 51. Were they successful in the communication attempts with extraterrestrials in that they got a reply and the meeting was planned by both parties? Or, were the communication attempts received by the ETs and they basically just showed up in response?

It was known, yes, as there had been two-way communication and that technology pointed to the fact there would be a landing at Area 51.

Earlier you said something that I must go back to. You said: "The visitors in this experience were of a further galaxy and this makes it *even more curious that the craft malfunctioned as it did*." Of course, this is a very good point. These ETs made it all the way from another galaxy only to make an error so close to a safe landing. That makes no sense at all. (It hasn't gone unnoticed by me how very clever you are with giving clues while insisting that I come to the thought and ask the question. I'm understanding your way: the golden path is a choice and we must seek to find and ask for it to be given.)

And this brings me to ask: Did the United States government crash the ETs' spaceship? Did they *deliberately* shoot down the craft?

Again, the greed and warring nature of your people caused them to react in fear and down the craft in order to steal its secrets regarding technology.

To welcome these visitors with love and acceptance would have brought full disclosure, as was their intention, but instead there was action of the lowest order by your military. *To live and act in fear is the lowest denominator of human interaction* and this was prominently displayed. It will never be completely known what might have come of this had there been an equal exchange of respect and knowledge.

It is a sadness to us that your society doesn't appear to have progressed far in the time since Roswell. At no time is there this type of behavior among other populations or the Universe in general. It is too clear to all that much soul-searching must be done, and change made amongst your civilization before you become a peaceful society to be welcomed else-where. You have the ability, but we do not consider you have the time or *will* to make yourselves over into a society in consideration of the bigger picture of maintaining the health of your environment now or where you may wish to relocate. You are where you are for now and until your higher thinking and acting is established.

Oh. My. Goodness. We crashed the spaceship at Roswell. *We crashed the spaceship at Roswell!*

This is a terrible, terrible shame. And, I'm baffled at the timing of the formation of the United States Air Force which was established as a separate branch of the U.S. Armed Forces in September of 1947; the Roswell incident occurred four months earlier in June of the same year.

Additionally, coincidental (or not) it is that the first surface-to-air missile (SAM) went up around 1947 and by 1950, SAM tests and launches were in full swing. I wonder (as historians might wonder) if the SAM was made after and as a result of the encounter at Roswell or if it *was* the weapon that took down the ET craft. You said that this ET visitation was known to the U.S. military, and so my question is: Was the U.S. military mak-ing preparations in advance of the ET visitation, planning in a way for this event?

As it was known this visitation was to take place, so was it known that it would be useful to take down one of the visitor craft for the purpose of taking the secrets to how it functioned. Your Earth people were not nice, at the time, about things such as this. They functioned in fear and this is what informed their decision-making process pertaining to the Roswell visit.

Premeditated, it was, and this is the reason why no further interest in visitation to Earth exists on the part of peaceful inhabitants of other host planets.

Oh my.

Did the home-planet people of the ET visitors know what happened—that this crew was shot down? Was there a way that this information was communicated all the way back to their home peoples? Or, did they just go missing and mysteriously never returned home?

Theirs was not the only ship arriving at that time, therefore the outcome was known to their home people. Communication between them is instant, as thought, therefore your way of considering how they could or would transmit this news differs from their reality. There was knowledge of the event, yes.

This is something that I missed or didn't ask: there was more than one spacecraft involved in the Roswell incident. How many crafts were there that day? Two, three … a dozen?

Eight crafts in all intended to stop but not all did, of course.

Apart from the craft that was shot down, did the other seven crafts just leave Earth that day and return to their home planet? They didn't fire back? Did they try to help their fallen team members, or did they instantly exit when our people became violent?

The small fleet that was present was planning to visit—this became a non-event when the military intervened and the rest is history. Their way is to not interfere in a situation such as this, not retaliate, and at that time their protocol was to depart immediately. Those other visitors left the area.

I'd love to imagine what they look like. I can't ask about the appearance of *all* extraterrestrials—given the wide variety of beings from many interstellar places—however, I would like to ask you about the appearance details of those beings who crashed at Roswell. This is one of those points of curiosity for our peoples and also it will be a revelation when this description matches the records that we will uncover in time about this incident. Therefore, what did the Roswell Alien Crew look like: how tall were they, what was the color of their skin, what was the shape of their head and eyes, and so on?

These details are well recorded by those who witnessed the event and we suggest no change to their descriptions of small body, large head and eyes. It is of no consequence now in your time.

We say that the visitors who came and stayed, *unintentionally*, were not alone. Others who come by are also similarly located while others from afar also keep watch. There will be opportunity to meet again and the full picture will become clear.

When?

At this time your people are not ready, nor will they be for generations, perhaps. There is no willingness on the part of off-planet visitors to make contact with those who would be hostile, fearful, warring, ready to monetize the event, and otherwise untrustworthy. These things your people currently are, and those who would make contact, especially.

Do the aliens have red blood like humans? (Some of our movies portray them as bleeding green. I guess we think of green when we think of aliens.) It's a novel question, yet I'd like to ask anyway.

Too much Hollywood we say. It matters not what color the inside when it is the outside that would not be accepted. Do you not find in your world today that you all bleed red, yet it is the exterior color that determines acceptance? Your people have far to go in realizing that eggs come in many colors but they are identical in the yolk.

Well said.
Did the Roswell ETs wear clothes—perhaps a space suit?

In their function as flight crew, there was need for specific attire, yes, and that was it.

Would they have been able to breathe our air, or would they have required their own breathing equipment for this visit?

Your atmospheric conditions were not a match for their needs so their ability included transport of what they did require should they leave their flight vehicle.

Had the crash not happened, how were they planning to communicate with earthlings? Could they speak English, or would they have used mind-communication, or would they have used a sign language of sorts as a universal communication tool?

Telepathic communication is their way. While they were capable of mimicking your language, it was not their choice to do so, but rather that those they communicated with should rise to the level of telepathy.

I've asked a lot about Roswell because it's America's most famous alien-encounter mystery. Interestingly, in doing an Internet search, I see that the overwhelming majority of UFO craft sightings are reported in the U.S.; more so than in Canada or Denmark or African countries, for example. Is there a reason for this? Are interstellar visitors more interested in the United States than other countries and areas around the world?

We will say that these fly-bys are in the areas mentioned not due to greater interest but as there is greater population density in the U.S. over Canada, thereby resulting in greater frequency of sightings. That is all.

The interest is in civilization on your planet, which is not determined by nationality. As we have previously stated, the visitors buzz by to see how civilization is progressing, *if* it is progressing in the broad sense of the word, and off they go.

People all over the world will read this and so I'd like to be equitable in my questions. If I were an extraterrestrial, I'd be doing quite a bit of buzzing by China and India—places densely populated and busy in their development of technology and communication modes. Yet, I couldn't find stories of ET or UFO sightings in those places. As you have said, the ET fly-bys are happening everywhere, but then, what's the

reason for little to no claims of sightings in these countries?

Ah yes, if it was technology that interested them, they would look in these places. However, whatever technology is there is quite primitive to the visitors.

When we say they buzz by to see how civilization is progressing, it is civil-ization in question. There is a use of this word in your language, being civil to one another meaning polite and helpful and non-threatening and reasonable in action. This is a gauge, not development of higher technology—for that they can provide guidance. As long as your peoples are warring and acting in ways designed to benefit self-interest not the greater good, it is a moot point how advanced in technology they are. If your leaders are corrupt, so are your people and if they are not corrupt but do not speak out against higher corruption, where is the division?

When we report the visitors see nothing they want so don't stay, it is into this morass of corporate and political corruption and greed they wish to avoid going. They do continue their watch, ever hopeful.

There was a claim of a UFO and two human-oid aliens spotted in 1965 by a farmer at Valensole, Alpes-de-Haute-Provence, France, and the event was dubbed as "France's Roswell". There was also a rumored close encounter of a UFO by another farmer in France in 1981 at Trans-en-Provence,

Var. May you please speak to these; were they truly alien crafts and beings?

While there was almost proof of the sighting in 1965, it became legendary for not becoming provable. Nevertheless, the local people believed something has been there that didn't belong.

In the later 1981 close encounter, it was just that, and was there something, or was there not? We say there was the belief strongly that the area had been disturbed by something other-worldly, but it was not to become fact.

While each was reported as an alien encounter, it was not so. For the local people to believe it was did not sit well with the military in the region and we say no further reporting was investigated.

UFOs are described as "flying saucers"; why are they disc-shaped?

You will note that they are not all disc-shaped—these differences are reported by those who see them on radar and, from higher in space, perhaps in close range. Aerodynamics will be a contributor to design, as will size requirement for specific use. Uses vary as do shapes and that is just the way of it.

Thank you for all of these details. I believe we've had a thought-provoking talk on historical alien encounters. I'm so very curious about it all and our readers will be, too.

Is there contact today from friendly interstellar visitors with the current United States government and/or other countries?

At this time in your U.S. government evolution, the friendly interstellar visitors you ask about are standing down from visitation for anything other than observation. It is a time on your Planet Earth— *globally*—that the energy of warring and negativity in general is bringing consternation, in a small way, to those who might visit, as they refrain and allow your people time to regroup and heal.

There can be no forward motion of a people when the people do not agree on the direction of that forward motion. It is a pivotal time for your future wellbeing.

Chapter Eight
Oil and Water

I'd like to explore some future technologies and advancements that can help our environment by replacing harmful methods and materials.

Carole recently mentioned to me over coffee that some decades ago you told her that people shouldn't be smoking tobacco, but rather we should be using it for our home insulation. May you please expand on that?

Ah yes, there are many uses for tobacco leaves, one of which is insulation against heat and cold.

What we said then was, "Focusing on tobacco use—it is a chief cause of decline in health for those of your world population and leads to the inhaling and taking in of other substances that harm the body and environment in other ways.

For the children to begin this evil is criminal; it should be removed from their sight, reach, and knowledge. Legislation against the sale and use of tobacco will be. It's hard for you to imagine this now, but it comes in the soon time.

Money derived from production and sale of tobacco is a large segment of the national income and is directed to politics in a big way. This connection is not lost on the people. Also not lost on the people is the need to put a stop to this, but how?

We ask for the industrial leaders to find another use for tobacco and the income will not cease, just originate from a different segment of the market. Has it been considered that tobacco leaves can be used for insulation in buildings? Find this connection and the next wave of invention begins.

Moving forward in time we say the non-smoking environment creates renewed health for all and the new uses of raw products keep happiness with the industry. It is a win–win situation."

You were right: this evolution of thinking and acting did come in the soon time. Much has changed and the non-smoking movement is vast, although too many still do smoke and we have not yet begun to invent new ways to utilize tobacco. However, I have a feeling that tobacco leaves for structural insulation will now be explored.

You said, "There are many uses for tobacco leaves, one of which is insulation against heat and cold." What are some of the other good uses?

Packaging for transportation of goods benefit from the insular properties of tobacco.

Okay, like for food service deliveries, medicine, and so on.

Also, there are rubber-like components to be found within the strands of the leaf and when associated with sporting equipment, uses can be beneficial. In shoes, particularly, there is a benefit and industry may begin to expand into this area.

You have me thinking of ski boots, winter gear, and more.
What is another resource that we're using the wrong way?

Hemp is underutilized. It is a natural resource and renews itself at a rapid rate. Those items now made of plastic type materials can be created through the use of hemp.

What is the reason this resource is being overlooked? Is there greed within the industry that allows the use of man-made materials as containers and other larger items that ultimately go into the landfills and oceans? We say there must be, and the time is now to investigate.

Hold the presses. So, everything that we are manufacturing using plastic can be made with hemp? Well, now, this will change things. From this day forward, if we could swap out all plastic (polluting and non-renewable petrochemicals: crude oil) with a hemp alternative (a rapidly

renewable natural resource) to create the same needed containers, tools, and medical equipment and such, much of our environmental pollution would *instantly* cease.

I've read that hemp is a carbon neutral material because it captures CO_2 as it grows and does so at a rate four times faster than trees. To hear that hemp can replace plastic is a huge tip.

So then, what *is* the reason that this resource is overlooked? It sounds like the truth runs deep and may be laced with nefarious ties, perhaps even with subsidies or other payouts and corporate codependency. Other than the manufacturing companies who make plastic, who else is benefiting from the perpetuation of the use of plastic and the continued pumping out of plastic products?

As the saying goes in your society, "Follow the money." It is rather like the pharmaceutical industry, yes? Your natural resources provide food and plants as medicine, but the majority shareholders in pharmaceuticals do not release this information.

Plastics remain the standardized use material for much in your society from containers to furniture to building materials. This has remained the go-to slice of society and now that ideas and attitudes are changing, it is time to know the resource of hemp growth is there. To mobilize the growers, to empower the growers is a beginning. Do they stand up to major manufacturers of plastics? Do they compete on an equal footing; a level playing field as it were? We say not in your today, but as they are empowered by society asking for alternatives, it will come to be.

We have the power, is what you're saying?

Do you know that all change begins with an idea followed by a voice and an intention? Yes, and this is the need now in your world before more time has passed. To blow open this information and share with those who care about distress in oceans currently covered with plastic is the beginning to change.

What this litter and plastic pollution is doing to fish and other water dwellers is just plain criminal, we say, as it need not be. What are you thinking, you manufacturers who know the error of your ways? We say you think of profit only—how do your children and grandchildren remember you if this is your legacy? For shame.

Now is the time to make amends to the Earth and society by offering to change your own manufacturing equipment to accept the raw material of hemp and transition your process. Now, don't you feel better about your contribution in this manner? Mother Earth thanks you.

As we are having this conversation, I did a quick Internet search for alternative materials to replace plastic and there are many suggestions

ranging from mushroom root to cornstarch. After some looking, I found that hemp is known to some and being used—although *not* widely—as a plastic alternative. I read about a company that uses cellulose from hemp to make products using a 3D printing technique. Is this the way? (It sounds like a winner to me.)

A process of forms and filling is simple enough using the liquefied cellulose product and is lower tech than 3D printing. The liquefied extraction of a hemp component, cellulose, will be pourable and malleable and an alternative to the artificial components of plastics. Also, it will return to Earth whereas plastic will not.

I'm also learning that there currently are "bio-plastic" products such as cups and other items that are made from vegetable fats, corn starch, woodchips, recycled food waste, and so on, that are labeled "biodegradable", "compostable", and "plant-based". And yet, there is rejection of these among some environmentalists for a couple of reasons: Firstly, it's said that they actually do not break down—not for many years. Secondly, if the bio-plastics accidentally end up in with plastic recyclable materials (due to similar appearance), they can ruin the batch of recyclables because they cannot be processed along with plastics.

How well and fast does hemp break down when it's used as a plastic alternative? And, is

hemp different or better than these other plant-based plastics that have been introduced?

As organic wastes are recycled for use as plastics alternatives, and as hemp is included in the configuration of the material make-up, so it can become a new and organic material which will satisfy environmentalists as to its ability to be strong in use but return to earth when discarded. The use of these materials together ensures a fully recyclable product with no fear of contamination of any sort. There are fears of the unknown here, and so long as manufacturers do so with ethical intentions, all is well.

The hemp is but one organic material, as has been mentioned, and its organic nature fits the profile of worthy components and it is the case that other seed and nut byproducts contribute their strengths and fibers to the equation and the end result is strength and clarity and the ability to degrade in recycling or composting even: both are required for variety of consumer uses.

There are popular tourist attractions frequented by organized tour groups, where, as part of their travel packages, the tourists are given water bottles throughout their day of sightseeing. These water bottles are distributed by the millions every day, and many of these countries either don't have recycling policies, or the bottles just end up in the trash, regardless. Every single

day, millions upon millions of water bottles go directly into landfills. Imagine if all of the companies that make plastic water bottles changed over within a year's time to using hemp for manufacturing instead. That one change alone would make a tremendous difference in the global pollution crisis. Is it a fairly easy and likely shift to seamlessly move from plastic to hemp?

Wholesale shifts like this are not easy from an economic perspective. It must be shown that costs are workable and that the resource is plentiful, and also that the public rejects the notion of continued plastics use. Like plastic bags being rejected, this is a target to remove plastic bottles. It is the users to target. The bottled water companies who purchase them, the drink manufacturers who purchase them by the millions—these are the targets for selling the idea of a renewable resource that grows at a rapid rate, not a chemically based plastic. Public demand and public rejection are powerful incentives in corporate decision-making.

In addition to plastic's payload of environmental pollution, there are the health impacts of our daily contact with plastic that we spoke of earlier. Plastic is used to make everything from the cups we drink from and the containers we store our food in, to the teething rings, bottles, and bottle nipples that our babies suck on, to the toys we play with from infancy through adulthood, and even those that our pets chew on. There are some brands of individual tea bags that are made from plastic which inevitably shed plastic fibers into our drinks; it's everywhere. Not to mention, polyvinyl chloride (PVC) is widely considered the most toxic of plastics, and yet it's a building material that runs throughout our living space like veins. We seem to know that chemicals in plastics can leach into our foods and drinks, and yet we're still using them and serving them up to our beloved children who are too young to decide if they want that poison in their systems. Oh, crikey, and yes—think of medical plastics like IV bags and what is really being pumped into the veins of our sick!

Beyond plastic in contact with food, may you please speak plainly to the health ramifications of our plastic use?

It is the sadness of your time that duplicity exists to the extent it does. Why do your people put heads in sand and not acknowledge danger where they know it to be? Is it for convenience of the consumer and growth of wealth for the manufacturer? Why is there no disclosure of truth? Even as your pharmaceutical industry discloses potential side effects of drugs, which, if truly listened to and understood, would shock and scare the average person away from their use, but it does not. It is a time of ostriching, we say, and your humanity has no chance of survival while in this position.

Do you wait to be told what is to be next in your journey to planetary wellness? Do you not act until told how to act? You have past civilizations and cultures that succumbed to this ostriching and leadership took a dark turn, as did the behaviors or lack thereof sometimes, of followers. It was a dark time and a sad time and a seemingly to-be-repeated time. Woe unto those who plant head firmly in sand while the way to survival is being shown.

Plastics use is one area of your time that will be read about in history books and not understood by the enlightened societies to follow.

It is shameful and toxic and the off-gassing from plastics in household use is of a high level, one that shows itself in increasing toxicity and dis-ease amongst your peoples. Do not think that chemical imbalances in the brains of children are unrelated. When did the epidemic of this become noticed— was it coinciding with the wholesale replacement of glass with plastic in your homes? Think on this, people.

We have many issues to tackle and you are gifting us with the wisdom to do it. I'm sure you know of the two gargantuan floating islands of plastic rubbish currently in the north central Pacific Ocean. We're very aware of them; we've even given them names: "The Great Pacific Garbage Patch", which includes the "Eastern Garbage Patch" between Hawaii and California, and the "Western Garbage Patch" between

Hawaii and Japan. Oil (plastic) and water don't mix (or shouldn't), so let's look at it.

I've read that while some people are thinking up ways to collect these islands out of the ocean, we don't currently have a good plan (or perhaps the resource or interest) to successfully do so. Do you have a suggestion from the Spirit World?

There is the awareness of plastic collection floating processing platforms currently in use on your oceans. They have been developed in recent times and are making a difference now, however more of these floating platforms are needed to be created and deployed around the globe. They were developed in your western world and available with enough funding to produce and purchase. Their evolution is underway and yet the current iteration is also very efficient and removes tons of plastics as it works.

All right let's see when these floating platforms are fully utilized, and the project is accomplished.

As we discuss water, it's in short supply on this planet and I don't understand why that is the case when I see oceans full of water. Why isn't desalinating saltwater to make potable water the solution?

Desalination methods exist and are in use but not widely on a large scale. We suggest to not think grandly of making fresh water from oceans using your *current method* of desalinization.

Yes, our known methods of desalination are distillation (water evaporation and condensing) and reverse osmosis (pushing water through a semi-permeable membrane, yet against water's natural tendency to equilibrate the minerals as opposed to removing them). Both methods are expensive. The former is expensive to heat and then chill the water, a downside that outweighs the benefits. And the latter requires a ton of electricity to push water through a filter. Although, in Kenya there is a pilot project that uses solar energy to power the desalination process.

What are we not considering as a solution to a lack of clean and drinkable water?

More focus is to be placed on preserving and increasing the fresh water that exists on the planet. How to accomplish this? It is a holistic approach, don't you know? You must preserve your forests and reforest where needed. The progression is reintroduction of wildlife to fill out the ecological system; birds and bees and wolves and beavers; herds of deer and grazing animals; fish returning through clean streams and rivers. Putting the land back into balance is key.

All imbalance causing climate change needs addressing; this is a beginning. None of it is effective in creating balance if air, soil, and water pollution continues at current rates. People of Earth, you have a choice to support future lives, or not.

It's better to fix what we have and what has, throughout time, sustained us and worked perfectly. You spoke before of systemic repair of our Earth ecosystems using the example of Yellowstone National Park and the total system imbalance when the wolves were killed off. It is enlightening to learn that ecosystem repair and balance is also an answer to the replenishment of our freshwater sources.

Out of curiosity, how do otherworldly advanced civilizations get their water?

Vapor catching and exchange is a common method. Life and needs are different as are requirements as you know them.

Maybe this can be applied to help some of us now?

What needs are on other planets are not Earth's needs, so focus where what is needed *already* exists.

Let's look at a place like California where the water supply shortage is considered critical; where the need for water cannot wait for a decade of ecosystem repair. How can they get more potable water in such places, faster than ecosystem repair will provide?

Other methods are in use now in your world and methods of cleaning saltwater to become clear and fresh water are well known (by some). It is for your people to advance the use of this technology to clean water in large quantities. You have water, California has ocean, and there is no reason to bypass this when technology exists.

Can you speak to the nature of this advancement in the technology of desalination?

The new way is a space-age technology in use currently to create clean water. Do some hold this close to themselves? Yes. Do some wish to share this with the developing world? Yes. Will it come to be that the technology is shared for humanitarian reasons?

We wish to encourage those with the power to release their methods for the survival of people, animals, and plants. Crops for feeding Earth are decimated in drought. It can be avoided.

Oh, Pax, this is important. I referenced California because I live in the United States, however the water shortage issue is much more dire in other places in the world such the major world cities of Cape Town and Mexico City, to name a couple.

This issue will become life-or-death for many. May you please further identify how saltwater can be made fresh? Do you have any out-of-the-box wisdom to share?

You have not considered the desalination *of old*.

A "neutralizer" exists that will clean ocean and all water of bacteria, dirt, chemicals, and render it suitable for sustaining life. It is found in nature and available to your people. It is an extract of tree soil, useful now and going forward *if it is harvested with respect for the land.* Think on this.

What kind of tree's soil; does it come from a particular tree? Does the tree give something off into the soil that is the magic ingredient?

Your forest floor provides nutrients dense in healing properties, especially in your old growth forests—another reason for preserving these sacred areas. Your First Nations people understand the breadth of healing properties found in nature and in these old groves of history-holding redwoods. The redwoods have watched your civilizations prosper and fail and return to try again, all the while cleaning the air and holding place for animals and birds in safety. What lies beneath and around them holds healing properties and, again we say, if harvested with respect for the land. This entails respect for standing trees, their roots and canopies, and careful extraction of appropriate for use amounts of soil.

Indigenous peoples and foresters are to be consulted.

Yes, you called them "*the wise-ones*"! The redwoods are only found in central California up through southern Oregon. Is this magical tree soil to be shared with other countries? While they have

lived for thousands of years, the redwoods live on land that today is designated national parkland, therefore "owned" by the U.S. government. I'm afraid that our people will not be able to resist stripping this resource to profit from it. Is there a way to reproduce the saltwater-purifying ingredient within the soil of redwood trees and therefore leave the redwoods be?

We say that as with many other developments, reverse engineering can accomplish this. The magic is in the soil and the accompanying and resulting magic is in the application.

Your engineers and scientists can extract for testing and consider the ingredient to duplicate. To share with the world, as and where needed, would be a goal.

Pax, do you know that this can change our world and save lives? Of course, you do. More than a billion people around the world lack access to clean freshwater (truthfully, California's water issue pales in comparison to the issue in countries like Yemen, Kuwait, Libya, Jordan, plus the Western Sahara and more); one third of the world's population experiences water scarcity at least one month per year, and for many it is every day of the year. Thank you. Thank you!

I feel like we need additional protective legislation in place beyond the existing Redwood Act (1978) before a single redwood is approached for

this purpose. Secondly, it sounds like we need to form a task force of indigenous peoples, foresters, engineers, environmentalists, and water specialists.

We are here to say the future comes in stages for your planet, both positive and negative, and this is the repeating of history. There is to be utmost concern now for your climate and ecology as it has been under attack for so long the recovery is perhaps not to be complete. It is never too late to begin the healing and we direct and encourage your Earth people to get on it, now.

As the air needs cleaning, begin with reduction of pollutants from chimneys and stacks heaving filth upward—for shame you should know this already.

The natural inclination of nature is to repair and re-grow when given opportunity, so stepping back from the harm-doing and allowing Mother Nature to take some deep breaths is the way. As a field lying fallow until the next planting allows the soil to rejuvenate, we ask you to expand this to all of the planet's soils and waters and air—just think on it and bring it down to smaller increments and begin.

To not be deterred by the perceived enormity of the task is the key. When we say waters, begin with one stream, one small rivulet and clean and protect.

Chapter Nine
Future Devices

*L*et's get a sneak peek at our tech devices of the future. I suppose we should begin with where we are now.

Along with all of our wireless devices today must also come a fair amount of electromagnetic field (EMF) radiation. In particular, we think of EMF from our cell phones and what this might be doing to our brains and organs as cell phones sit in our pockets and are held to our heads for sometimes hours every day. We suspect that cell phones are "frying" our brains, although we still use them. How harmful are cell phones to our brains?

The continual pressing of this current to the head is a fascinating trait of your people—it is not a wonder then that as user generations age there will be seen an influx of symptoms relating to early diminishment of mind-power as well as physical power. There is the relationship there that has resulted in debilitating the person in ways not previously seen.

Neurological connections can be traced and without doubt be pointed to cellular phone use as causative.

Some experts say that cellular networks such as 5G wireless communication emit powerful radio-frequency radiation and are sickening people, causing cancer and microwave-type burns, damaging DNA, and causing premature aging, etc. May you please speak to this technology and the "pressing of this current to the head," as you put it?

In the now is mass communication via cellular devices, satellites, and means that travel your words through and over wires and cords and wireless networks. This is a global mess, don't you know? Imagine your world without this electromagnetic mess cluttering the airways. And this is the way of the future.

There is to be clarity and not chaos, there is to be pure and intentional communication and not the messing with interruption of signals and pirating of messages and intentional barriers being set to willing and clear purposeful communication. At this time there are barriers to purity of intention as well as efforts to communicate those intentions globally. There are so many fences to climb and patterns which may be disrupted—it is a travesty now of pirating versus purity. Your world communication is a mess.

Recently, a friend tipped me off to a mineraloid stone mined from Russia called shungite. It

is claimed to provide protection from EMF radiation, and shungite patches for cell phones are now available. Yet, I've also read that shungite might have some negative side effects. Is shungite a useful material for EMF protection and what else can you tell us about EMF exposure as it affects our health?

Well now, this returning to the past to fix the future continues, yes? As this mineral is useful here you may also consider the damage done to mind and body from continual cellular telephone use. It is not just frying the brain that is problematic.

Oh, no? Do tell, please.

Combine that with the lack of awareness of the outside world in ways common to past times, consider the inability of children to converse and communicate with spoken words—this in itself is a travesty—then it is learned they are being poisoned by their devices. How uninformed can some people be through their own neglect of investigation. The shungite mineral itself is useful, not harmful, but contributes to the belief that harm is removed through its combination with electronics, while it is the electronics themselves contributing to the dissolution of wellness on your planet.

It becomes the easy way to plant a child somewhere with an electronic device to keep their attention; meanwhile it is a distraction rather than a learning tool when used this way. We anger at the picture of the next generation of learners becoming robotic in their need for electronics and lack of need for human interaction, in person. There should be limitations on use of behavior modifying devices—electronics.

For those who need to use a phone for business or to keep in contact with friends and family far away, is a shungite patch attached to our cell phone one small way that we can protect ourselves from EMF radiation?

Whatever is needed for self-protection is to be done, yes, and also the need for constant communication in this way is to be considered as questionable. There was a time when the need was not present and the world seemed to turn, as it should.

While we understand the need for instant gratification in most things among your peoples is high on the scale of needs, time will show that insufficient knowledge of what is accepted as required for successful and happy life may be not all of that in the long term.

Never mind, it is a sign of your times and this too shall pass.

There is something else coming to replace our current cellular phone technology—that's what you're hinting at, isn't it?

To function *as they are now intended*—there is an alternative, yes, and it involves a design modification that eliminates the way charging is managed.

Cellular technology has not considered the health connection in development of power sources. There is no need for this always-on way of being.

Well, well, well: a cell phone charging modification. I'd like to wrap my mind around how this alternative charging would be done: how does it work, Pax?

One development that will be of interest is a considered power source that takes into account the personal health and wellness of a chronic user—it is to be addressed. It is the use of the method of charging that will change with the type of battery installed. The need for electricity to charge is replaced with light such as solar—it is a beginning and options abound. This is the place of where your satellite communication remains the way, and these signals will be received and replace the battery as you now know it. This method revolutionizes the industry as current battery types can be problematic and cause damage to not only health and wellness, but also environment. Greater global dependency on connecting is answered in this manner.

Change comes and you will approve.

I can just see all of our experts in communications technology working more rapidly on these new directions.

What is the next evolution in replacement of current cell phone technology?

Communication in your soon time looks different from your now, and in your far time does not require external devices. Think on this.

We have stated the way of your future is telepathic communication and this is what you shall work towards.

This is exciting, to say the least.

Penelope, moving ahead in time, we see the communication method being telepathic alongside tiny instruments that do all for you. Understand that this is acceptable and in the soon time come prototypes of what will be then common. It is the best of times and it is understood that commonsense is required with advances, and to understand those that will benefit mankind and instill in each other the knowledge that less is more in terms of equipment.

Can you tell us more about these tiny instruments that do all for us? What do they do for us? Do they work like a cellphone in that they operate by an electrical signal transmitted by radio waves?

These tiny instruments as we have called them are what you will use for communication and programming of all your earthly needs by satellite transmission. You will not only communicate with each other your plans and movements but advise your means of transportation and your household gadgets what you want of them, and when. It is a command post, if you will, that you speak to and the voice recognition takes it from there. It is your way to make all life movements trackable and all needs monitored via this device which fits into the palm of your hand or is wrapped around an arm or wrist or hung on a belt—it is the object that manages all life needs.

You will be glued to it.

Does this device also evolve—as it seems that all technology does—and if so, what will its future become?

One day it can be so tiny as to be implanted under skin and you will not need the external device. Each person will be chipped for identification and this device is also a transmitter and receiver for communication. It is useful for all things you presently carry in your wallet and cellular telephone and replaces all. It's quite simple, really, but speaks to a higher level of control if utilized incorrectly. It is intended to simplify life.

If the device were to be imbedded under our skin, how would we operate it and interface with it?

Telepathically is the way, as it will be for all things.

It will be mobilized by a thought command as your instruments of today are in speaking a command to contact a person or open a door or activate music, all pre-programmed and some not, but voice-activation of today becomes thought-activation of tomorrow.

Wowzers.

Do you approve or disapprove of the chip under skin?

It seems a natural progression and the inner-strength and knowing of how to function in these times becomes a glorious quest for many. This is the way of your future and the determination is if *you* approve.

We understand it is to be, and that when used for pure purposes will benefit your people. As with reality there are nefarious purposes of control that could be enacted. Your people will understand this and have options for the use of their personal chip—you approve it and you control it. We state it is to be the way and that is the story.

The micro-chipping of humans is something of which we've heard and read. This concept of chipping everyone would replace everything from paper currency, to medical records, to tax filings, and criminal records, etc. It would basically

hold all records and identification of each person. Many people say this is what was described in Revelation in the Bible as the "sign of the beast", and "the anti-Christ".

Was this the chipping forewarned in Revelations? And, is this story in Revelations true or did we misinterpret it?

As you understand that the Bible book was rewritten more times than were counted and interpreted by those writing at the time, this story was the equivalent of the present-day science-fiction tale. Many ideas were visualized and considered while the influence of outside was in action—this is one and while visionary, is not to be feared.

If this story is to be believed by your people, it should be understood you will have generations of "beasts" and "anti-Christs" to come. Interpret that.

Hmmm. I'd best leave that for our theologians. On a somewhat related topic, what do you think about globalization?

Consider the big picture and one's neighbor country or continent as to be respected and protected. To live locally in terms of commerce and agriculture is meaningful to the future of Planet Earth. It is time to scale back the reliance from afar when the way of self-sufficiency has been discarded. This came of a lazy attitude and is now to be replaced with reliance on self and community.

A reversal of the ways of purchasing and giving away of personal power is to begin. This must now revert to self-empowerment with your people, a regaining of your confidence in your ability to provide and succeed.

Rely on yourselves for your future—it is your power to reclaim.

$$\bullet \; \bullet \bullet \; \infty \; \bullet \bullet \; \bullet$$

About the Author and Channeler

*P*enelope Jean Hayes is a new consciousness author, television personality, and speaker. She has appeared on-camera hundreds of times as an expert guest on programs including *Dr. Phil*, *ABC News*, as well as international news specials and telecasts. She is the foremost leader in the field of contagious and osmotic energy known as Viralenology, founder of the Viral Energy Institute, and author of the book *The Magic of Viral Energy: An Ancient Key to Happiness, Empowerment, and Purpose.*

Carole Serene Borgens channels Pax, the Divine Wisdom Source. Carole is a former nurse and longtime student of metaphysics. She has been channeling Spirit since the early 1990s when she was chosen by Pax and given the title "Spirit Messenger". Carole continues to write and provide in-person and remote sessions for clients around the globe, and she refers to her gift of channeling as "the greatest blessing in my life."

Of this trio, Pax says, "A good team we three."

www.PaxWisdom.com
www.PenelopeJeanHayes.com
www.CaroleSereneBorgens.com

www.ingramcontent.com/pod-product-compliance
Lightning Source LLC
Chambersburg PA
CBHW031527040426
42445CB00009B/437